WHEELS OF CHOICE

WHEELS OF CHOICE

Tim Hughes

Cyclographic
Publications

First published 1980 by Cyclographic Publications
Great Missenden, Buckinghamshire HP16 0HD

Copyright © 1980 W.T. Hughes

ISBN 0 907191 00 2 (casebound)
ISBN 0 907191 01 1 (paperback)

Printed and bound in Scotland by Clark Constable Ltd,
Edinburgh

Chance and choice

In 1896 H. G. Wells's Mr Hoopdriver, freed for a week from his humdrum job, took to the bicycle and the open road. Wells's novel *The Wheels of Chance* tells how they led him to romance and the encounter with the Girl in Grey. For Mr Hoopdriver and millions of others the bicycle became a passport to a different world, an escape from everyday bonds into an unknown and largely rural landscape. For me, too, the bicycle was the means by which my horizons were extended from the small village where I grew up. It has been the bicycle that directly and indirectly has taken me to a variety of countries to meet a wide range of people - through choice. But chance comes in even here. It was a fortunate chance for me that my parents introduced me to the machine which had given them in their turn so much pleasure. Chance in weather, in lighting, in the groupings and expressions of people, has helped with many of the pictures in this attempt to put over some of the contrasting types of enjoyment that can be found with the aid of the bicycle. I find it amazing to look back over my three hundred thousand and more varied cycling miles and realise how many were not wholly by choice but dictated by having to get to work or other places, or just as certainly but more subtly by the need to work off the competitive urge. However, the wheels that brought me to the places where these pictures became possible were, for me, special ones. They took me where, when and how I wanted - they were my Wheels of Choice.

About the photographs

When I first embarked on this project I thought that the pictures would fall easily into categories - people, places, seasons, countries and so on - and that these would define the chapters. Or perhaps the sequence would follow a typical year, a distillation of all the years (it's been done before) from spring to winter. But the more I looked at the pictures, shuffled them, thought of the memories they evoked and the words they would need, the more obvious it became that they wouldn't stand these formal divisions. So that is why they follow a not-quite-random pattern - that of a series of anecdotes, happenings and chance meetings.

The life of a cycling photographer riding with other cyclists can be hard. If he wishes to photograph his companions on the move, he must forge on ahead to a likely spot, take a chance on their inadvertently assuming grotesque poses or breaking the rules of the road as they pass - or even on their taking an entirely different route. Then he must pack his bag and chase to catch them up again, ready for the next go. Photographs at planned and unplanned stops are easier, provided the ingredients of picnic lunches or toolkits aren't spread too haphazardly over the landscape. I would like to have been able to claim that all the photographs in this book were true captured moments of this nature, with the photographer selecting but not influencing. But this is not a perfect world and some of the pictures *are* posed, the 'models' sometimes *did* repeat the action just once more for the cameras, or were even led to a location spotted on an earlier cycle ride and which offered possibilities for conveying a particular atmosphere. I don't think it shows too much. And it is to my largely uncomplaining models that this book is unhesitatingly dedicated.

Other cycling photographers may be interested that sixteen different cameras were used - not for any particular reason but because they were there! About two-thirds of the original negatives and transparencies were in the 6 x 6cm size and the remainder nearly all 35mm. Perhaps the preponderance of rollfilm reflex camera negatives explains why I find it so hard catching up again ...

Some of these photographs are old personal favourites and have been reproduced before - often drastically cropped to fit editorial requirements - in *Cycling, Cycletouring, Bicycle Buyers Guide* and a few in my own *Adventure Cycling in Britain* and other books. Most, however, are published here for the first time and are reproduced in the format in which they were originally envisaged.

Finally, cycle-tourists are obsessively curious about place - if you showed them a picture of the first authentic space ship to land from an alien planet they'd peer at the background, crying in triumph: 'That's Pen-y-Ghent!' or 'Boston Stump!' or whatever. Pages 94 and 95 therefore give details of where the pictures were taken.

The bicycle, in all its guises, has a wholly distinctive outline. From the most amazing distances the two simple circles of the wheels, in substance or in shadow, proclaim 'this is a bicycle'. These shapes catch and hold the eye, whether they belong to the most luxurious of hand-built machines or to a neglected workhorse like this one, parked against an Artois cottage wall in the heat of a July noon.

Mounted, the shape of the cyclist is just as distinctive, no matter how it is disguised or even when it is seen from so far away that riders are no more than ants on a vast landscape. Dismounted, cyclists with their bicycles are still cyclists. I couldn't resist this chance encounter between a couple walking uphill and these alien beings - male and female road signs from a past age.

The open road: the ultimate cycling cliché - but at the same time not so very far from the ultimate cycling truth. Many would ask no more than this French scene offers: a gently undulating and curving road to an undiscovered destination, sunshine and a few congenial companions.

But if the general outline of the cyclist is easily spotted, you have to admit that they do come in all shapes and sizes. Together with these goes an almost infinite variety of postures on and off the machine - each an individual imprint, making silhouettes of members of a group instantly recognisable to their friends.

Almost a family album. The hard-used sidecar was third-hand when we bought and rebuilt it - and I

suppose you could say sixth-hand by the time we passed it on! The special child-back tandem, too, bought for a fiver and renovated, saw the whole family through - and in the end sentiment won and we didn't sell it! But time passes quickly and it's not long before yesterday's sidecar passengers have bicycles of their own.

From here on we set out on a variety of journeys to an equally wide variety of places. And what place better to begin, with a young companion, than on the broad grassy springtime rides of Thetford Forest, the biggest tract of English woodland south of Carlisle.

The theme of 'cyclist in landscape' will predominate in the pages to come for if there's one thing the leisure cyclist is always conscious of, it's the immensity of the countryside and the power of the elements. It is impossible not to feel dwarfed - but not belittled - by towering mountains and the thin winding line of the road scratched on the hillside. Equally the great dome of a Fenland sky and the horizontal openness of such a landscape are impressive indeed.

Then as we shall see, the finer points emerge. The scenes on the next two pages seem almost etched in their detail. The individual cherry trees stand out white against the almost leafless early spring background of the steep-sided River Orne valley in Normandy. A month or two earlier in the year the Brecon Beacons show one of their harsher moods. The few pines and wind-torn heather stand out black against the pale tones of the frozen lake and the snow. It is not sunshine but the varying depth of snow whipped up by the wind that outlines the shapes of the gullies on the far hillside.

A bright interval as the sun makes a brief appearance on a winter trip to the Towy valley. South and mid-Wales have always been firm favourites and the Towy valley one of the high spots. Now the old track has gone, much of it drowned beneath the new Llyn Brianne. In its place, raw as yet but rapidly mellowing, is a new road which plunges, twisting and climbing spectacularly round the artificial lake's many inlets. Together with the more recent forestry this is hill farming country: from spring to autumn the hills are alive with the soft but plaintive call of distant sheep. Otherwise it's open and lonely.

Further north, the Scottish landscapes on pages 26 and 27 show two contrasting views of the country - the long sea arm of Loch Fyne and the bare hillsides of the Southern Uplands.

From the wilder uplands we return to the more intimate countryside of the south. Man has controlled this landscape for centuries. In many parts the harmonious blending of land and village architecture - making sympathetic use of indigenous materials - is one of the main attractions.

The landscapes of East Anglia are often dismissed as flat and uninteresting but for the cyclist prepared to use a map to seek out the network of minor roads that cross the region there are many rewards. Even if they do not compete with grander mountains, parts of Norfolk, Suffolk and Essex can be unexpectedly hilly. The variety of landscape and the many rivers mean that you can one minute be following an avenue of poplars, the next travelling along a narrow corridor between waist-high fields of ripening corn - and then be brought to a halt at the water's edge where the ferry waits.

On this particular weekend to north Suffolk and Norfolk we had encountered them all. It was at the end of August and after buying our weekend's food from the stalls of Downham Market a brisk breeze had borne us beneath fleecy white clouds across the fertile Fens to the banks of the River Ouse at West Lynn. The map marked a ferry but we had our

doubts, since ferry services are withdrawn far quicker than maps wear out. However, not only was there a ferry to Kings Lynn but it was prospering as returning local shoppers took this chance of avoiding the heavy traffic over the only bridge into the town. The day was rounded off by one of those utterly enjoyable but unspectacular journeys over a rolling landscape golden with wheat and oats, punctuated by the pine and birch of the forests around Sandringham.

Woodland features in the next few pages and the season moves on from high summer into autumn - and from a track through a rather untypical Chiltern birch wood by way of a mid-morning halt in Derbyshire to a bright autumn afternoon above Brecon.

Some of the most enjoyable cycle-touring is to be found well away from the popular holiday season, when there's a chance to see places in a different and more relaxed mood. For several years we have made short trips of a few days at the end of October - a season when the weather can be surprisingly mellow, as in this scene near Kirkby Stephen. The season progresses and the weather sharpens on the next two pages, leading us into winter.

If autumn is colourful, then cycle-touring in winter is cycling at its most dramatic. Maybe it's something to do with a south-country upbringing, but snow-covered hills have always lured me - right from our first acquaintance. That was when, as two sixteen-year-olds, we had ridden some 160 miles on a cold Good Friday up to north Wales. The weather had not been kind: hail and sleet showers had buffeted us and the wind had been fickle. And experienced cyclists will feel a cold shudder of recollection at the thought of repeatedly donning and doffing a cold wet cape on a long hard journey. Anyhow, we arrived weary at dusk at Llangollen with only another few miles to do. But my companion's bicycle - and he too - had had enough and both ended up in the shelter of a police station to await the opening of a cycle shop in the morning. I continued the journey alone. The moon was full: the sky had cleared and it was a sharp frosty evening. Suddenly, as I rounded a bend on the road to Corwen, there ahead of me, silver in the moonlight, was the first snow-capped mountain I had ever seen. From that moment I was beyond rescue. So now, every mid-February, we set out for a long weekend to the winter hills in the search for snow. Over the years - in mid, south and north Wales, the Peak District and Yorkshire - we have had some superb experiences, not without some disappointments too. But at its best, as on the magnificent weekend in the Brecon Beacons and Black Mountains on these few pages, the beauty of sun on snow on mountains is breathtaking. Snow can disguise an undistinguished landscape, fill in the quarries and roadworks and restore a pristine clarity of line and tone to a ravaged hillside.

Of course mileages are restricted and the going is sometimes tough but when I spoke of 'disappointments' I meant the weekends when there was no snow - not that there was too much. Some of the perversely spring-like occasions have naturally been eminently enjoyable, but they weren't *real* winter weekends!

Our first winter weekend over fifteen years ago: just below the snow line on the south side of Cader Idris, looking out over Craig-yr-Aderyn -the 'Bird Rock' - near Abergynolwyn. In this picture on the left, Jack's face and figure feature often in these sunlit winter pictures but even as a hardened winter-weekender I don't think he'd have been smiling quite as broadly on page 46 if he'd known that we were about to embark on the long foggy trek over the Black Mountains which followed.

There was certainly no doubting the wintriness of this weekend as Jack, again, faces the blizzard on the slopes of the Brecon Beacons. The track, snow-filled and impassable, lies to the left and it was easier going across the wind-blasted moorland. The previous day had been one of high drama on the Roman road over the Beacons, glacier-like at the top, with a gusty wind whipping the snow into whirling columns. At night, in the relative shelter of Llwyn-y-Celyn, a fine haze of sparkling and dancing ice-crystals hung in the air as the wild bitter wind shook the stout walls. In the morning thin drifts of fine snow curled into the room from every cranny in the doors of the old farmhouse. A winter weekend indeed.

Now, you can't plan for everything. The place is right, the Bwlch-yr-Efengyl in the Black Mountains, the weather is right - but it's *not* a winter weekend. In fact it's the aftermath of an April shower gone wild one Easter.

The call of the winter hills this time comes from the north, from the Craven area of Yorkshire. We had started out from Skipton and soon left the Aire valley to head up into the limestone hills towards Malham. The morning greyness had given way to a

brilliant afternoon. The season was at that delicate balance where in the sheltered valleys all the signs of spring are present but a thousand feet higher on the fells the snow still lies quite thickly. Once through Malham and up the stiff climb which leads up towards Malham Tarn it was a different world of whiteness. Away eastwards from the Tarn swept the twin walls bounding Mastiles Lane, a grey serpentine double line pointing the way to Kilnsey. In summer the old grassy track is crowded - and often very boggy underfoot, or underwheel. But on this February afternoon it was deserted and firm, a compelling invitation. Eventually the five miles of trackway drop to the metalled road of Littondale and we had the reward, as the brief winter afternoon came to an end, of watching the upper slopes of Pen-y-Ghent and Fountains Fell turn a brilliant crimson under the rays of the setting sun before we hurried down to Stainforth for food and shelter for the night.

One of the most striking features of the hills in winter is the utter silence. However peaceful, a summer landscape is seldom quiet. There is always the sound of water tumbling, of leaves rustling or of sheep calling - even where there are no man-made sounds. But in winter the leaves have gone, snow covers the grass and the sheep have been taken down from the high fells to more secure pasture or shelter in the valleys. Even the mountain stream can be stilled by a sharp frost and you then have that rarest of modern opportunities, that of silence - provided you can persuade your companions to be still and share it.

As we've seen in several pictures already, a useful time to catch a couple or small group of cyclists is when they've paused for a few moments to check on the map. It's a useful 'pose' photographically, because it's one of the few occasions when two or three people spontaneously concentrate on a single object without any concern for the camera. Indeed, if they're worried enough about their geographical position, they may well ignore the photographer completely. Additionally, the light reflecting surface of the map throws light up into the shadows of the face - it all seems too neat a solution to be true!

But cycle-tourists do use maps for other than motives of sympathy for photographers. The map is the most useful tool the exploring cyclist has for seeking out pleasant and interesting variations of route; of, as it were, attempting deliberately to stumble on the unexpected. Without a map we would never have been intrigued by the winding road on the other bank of the Dordogne, opposite the obvious route. And then we would never have discovered the fascination of the sun-bleached alleyways and arched entries of the village of Carennac, a superb and almost unsung gem. Sometimes, however, it does seem difficult to open a map without help pouring in from all sides demanding to know if, or even more probably assuming that, you are lost. Always excepting those occasions when you really *are* lost, of course. The map is essential, too, if you're going to leave the literally beaten track, when you can soon find yourself in the position of the 'rider' on page 59. Even so, was he there because of the map - following an intriguing and inviting path - or in spite of it?

Because the fuel which powers the cyclist is food, the topic is a major one in the cycle-tourist's life. It takes on not only a very practical desire for food and drink but an aesthetic one as well. I have known the search for an ideal picnic spot begin soon after midday and stretch deep into the afternoon, long after the pangs of hunger had become a gnawing urgency. We were lucky on this October day that a mile or two after stocking up at Arkholme we crossed this old bridge over the River Lune and saw a sunlit meadow at the water's edge below us.

Of course you can buy a midday meal and most cycle-tourists' repertoires of memories are full of stories of gastronomic delights found in inns and small villages: I think I would describe the corner of Oakham on page 62 as as true-to-life a cycling picture as you'll find. However, no tour, no weekend, no foray into the hills would be complete or even possible without the halt at the village shop to buy food for an open-air lunch.

And the picnic allows the photographer free rein once more, for if the map-reading cycle-tourists were concentrating on their subject, how much more are these.

If the lunch spot combines practical advantage with aesthetic desirablility then so much the better. The forest clearing in Norfolk and the wall in Lancashire both gave shelter from the wind. Cyclists' lunches are the same the whole world over: no European would fail to recognise the

preparations by the side of Lake Yamanaka with a cloud-topped Mt Fuji in
the background. Equally the brief pause in the shade beneath the birch
tree is universal in its meaning. But what are we to make of the cycle-
tourists on page 68, calmly picnicking as though it were Box Hill in midsummer?

Undoubtedly one of the joys of cycle-touring is the ability to stop. Not to stop because the rhythm of movement is in any way unenjoyable in itself - although even the most doggedly diehard traveller needs eventually to stop for rest - but to stop to look. The bicycle confers the gift of seven-league boots on the self-propelled but at the same time allows the cyclist to pause almost at a whim, with few practical parking problems. Equally the bicycle, on its way at a reasonable human speed, enables its rider to espy detail in the hedgerow, the village or town, the distant momentary vista, that a faster traveller cannot.

The unusual or the remarkable catch the eye. For some it is the rare or unexpected flower, for others the detail of construction of a cottage or some relic of the past. It would be here that I, too, should claim some special intellectual or praiseworthy interest in what I notice from the saddle but, alas, it seems that it is mostly the incongruous, the banal and the ephemeral that catch my attention. It might be the utterly unsuitable house name - an idyllic country cottage with the appropriate roses round the door named after some unsalubrious city suburb, or the stockbroker-belt house set in four acres and labelled 'Something Croft'. Perhaps I can claim more credit for noticing the intangible among the ephemeral - the fleeting glint of light on water, the sudden changes in temperature on a still autumn evening as the road dips and climbs, and the cooking smells as the last miles of the evening roll by. However, whatever the feature that takes the eye - or any other sense - the bicycle enables you to pause or pass at will.

Milestones have a particular place in the cycle-tourist's affections. They may seem to pass all too slowly at the end of a long day or into a head wind: their continental kilometric cousins may flash by on the speedy drop down a mountain pass. They may, like this one, be almost hidden and overgrown beside a narrow lane, remaining as the only evidence of former importance, or the sleepy villages that they name may show that they were erected at some eccentric squire's whim.

Our own country as we've seen offers an immense range of cycle-touring experience, within and without the accepted seasons. But almost every cyclist eventually wants to extend his experience to foreign touring. We begin our travels in Normandy, where we have spent several long weekends at Easter. The abiding memory of the green winding lanes of lower Normandy at that season will always be bank after bank of primroses, interspersed with the rarer cowslip.

Two glimpses of the different faces of cycle-touring in Poland. The occasion was one of the annual assemblies of cycle-tourists under the aegis of the Alliance Internationale de Tourisme, held that year at Sopot on the Baltic coast. Our small party had made the long journey by rail and sea to Poznań in the west of Poland, from where we were to ride, over several days, northwards to the sea.

This is not the spectacular part of the country, but a gently undulating and mainly agricultural landscape, later rising and giving way to birch forest as we rode into the hills of Pomerania. Maria, our guide, was worried when we decided to follow an attractive little road rather than the wide and well-surfaced but rather barren main one which went further round. She may have been right, for by the time we got to our journey's end for the day we had encountered several stretches like this one where opinions were divided as to which strip of sandy edge to follow to avoid the enormous irregular paving of the road itself.

Our impressions were of a very gentle

countryside, reminiscent of southern England before the war. Horses were being used to effect in bringing home the wheat harvest and field after field of golden grain was being gathered in. Small stalls in the rare villages sold enormous tomatoes. To wash away the dust of the hot dry days we would stop at a *piwarnia* - a small beer-house not unlike an isolated English pub.

Since this part of Poland is in the main not very heavily populated or industrialised, many of the bird species which used to summer in the Rhine valley now come here. Storks nest on farmhouse roofs, flying with a slow and dignified rhythm low over the marshes. We came on the birch forests almost unawares: over a space of a mile or two we moved from the corn-growing central European plain into surroundings that were almost Scandinavian, with brick and stone houses giving way to wooden cabins. We welcomed the shade of the trees as the previously flat roads began to climb and wind among the lakes of Kartuzy, before the final plunge to the Baltic.

I suppose that most of us would claim that, among other things we sought abroad, we went overseas to look for sunshine. This has certainly been true of the Easter holidays that we have spent in southern France, and we've usually been lucky.

But individual days have not always been so. On this Easter we had taken the train to Brive-la-Gaillarde in the valley of the Corrèze and then followed the valley of the Dordogne gently towards its source in the mountains of the Massif Central. We had decided to stop for a couple of days at Spontour on the Dordogne and to travel light into the hills for a day. After nearly a week of sunshine the day began wet and got colder and wetter as we climbed. We rode steadily up through Mauriac, across a few miles of a barren plateau and then dropped a little into the Vallée du Falgoux. Except for its larger scale we might have been in Wharfedale in Yorkshire and the chilling rain heightened the illusion.

It was by now well past midday and shelter for lunch was becoming urgent: We climbed slowly to the few houses and church of St Vincent - to find that it boasted not one café but two. One of the pleasant things about the best of French cafés, like the best of British pubs, is that they welcome in the traveller with food. No, said Madame, pushing two tables together so that all seven could dine as a group, there was no *dérangement*. Yes, we could dry our wet gloves round the stove: yes, we could have two bottles of a *vin du pays*, a mineral water and a litre of soft drink to be followed by seven coffees. Would we care for the local newspaper, and was there anything else we would like? The total bill came to just under a pound.

When we came out the rain had stopped and a fitful sun followed our progress up to the snow line on the Pas de Peyrols, rewarding us with a golden evening for our final descent to the Dordogne.

Let us not dwell too long on bad weather, however. Our next trip abroad takes us to Champagne, for a weekend based on Reims. Every year the local cycle-touring club, the Groupement Champennois Cyclotouriste, organises its Randonnée de la Montagne de Reims.

This event brings together two or three thousand cyclists to follow a choice of routes around the woods and vineyards of the 'Montagne' de Reims. The range of chalk hills, some 900ft at their highest, bear on their slopes most of the famous vineyards from whose grapes is made the sparkling wine. From early in the morning the streets of the city are alive with little groups of riders setting out on circuits from 30 to 150km.

The day soon warmed up from a chilly start and we made our leisurely way through neat geometric rows of ripening vines on the sunlit slopes, then swooped into the welcome shade of beech and oak woods. All the routes converged on the little village of Rilly-la-Montagne where the whole village square had been taken over to serve riders with a picnic lunch and, of course, champagne. It seemed somehow appropriate that the road back to Reims should be lined by vineyards ...

Inevitably the cycle-tourist eventually succumbs to the lure of the high mountains, for it is there that the greatest personal challenges and the greatest personal rewards are to be found. I have tried to put this into words before but it seems almost impossible without sounding falsely pious to put over what is no less than a kind of spiritual uplift that keeps pace with the road as it winds higher and higher. To the non-cyclist, spending a holiday in riding uphill on a bicycle seems a contradiction in terms, at its mildest. And there's no doubt that riding uphill is quite hard physical work - which can be eased by the right equipment - and it's also true, seeing how short a time it takes to come down, that a large proportion of the time of a mountain crossing is spent in climbing. Naturally the highest mountains in general offer the greatest thrills, although many would agree that some of the minor Alpine passes, perhaps a little lower than their celebrated and often main-road rivals, offer the greatest thrill of all.

A typical day in the mountains starts early, if you are to make the best of the day. It will almost certainly be summer or early autumn, since it is only at this time that the very highest roads in the Alps and Pyrenees are open after the winter snows.

The valley will probably be in shadow as you set out but the sun will already be well up on the high peaks of which you get tantalising glimpses as the road turns. Perhaps remnants of the night's mists will still be swirling about the very tops. The valley may well lie in a forest and a noisy stream is almost certainly tumbling alongside the road. You climb steadily and the lowland trees give way to pines and birches, while the roadside flowers give the impression that you are moving back through the season to an English spring. The trees begin to thin and you find yourself in harsher, barer country. The stream is smaller now and the road begins to wind, doubling back on itself as it tries to cross the slope at a gentle angle. With every turn the glimpses of the peaks become longer and more turns of the road come into view. Then, high above you in a cleft you see the cross or isolated refuge that marks the top. Your goal is in sight and each hairpin now brings you closer to the top instead of further from the bottom. Finally the last few metres to the top and there spread before you is a new landscape: glancing back you see that just as splendid a view has developed behind you, a literal panorama. You are on the roof of your world.

In your desire to get to the highest passes, though, do not neglect the foothills. Some of the most attractive climbs are here and they are accessible for much longer in the year. Typical of the best are the regions which border the southern valley of the Rhône in France - the Préalpes and the Vercors to the east and the mass of gorges and uplands that make up the Ardèche to the west.

These are heavily wooded areas, although many of the trees which make up the cover are found in Britain only under cultivation. In early summer, before the heat of July and August has dried them up, they are a mass of shades of green, varied by the yellow of laburnum and the often vivid colours of the rocks - reds, golds and the almost steely blues of volcanic types - contrasting here and there with the bleached white of the predominant limestone.

The climbs are shorter than the classic routes of the Alps and their summits may be a thousand metres lower but they can be in their way just as dramatic - and frequently much more colourful. It is perhaps on the descents that the difference is most marked. On the major passes of the Alps and Pyrenees the sheer exhilaration of freewheeling often so grips the mind that the effect of the surroundings is overwhelmed. It gets to all of us: I know plenty of people who'll take photographs going up a pass but not many who'll stop on the way down. The rush of the wind, the swooping round the bends and the gentler curves of the route are almost sufficient of themselves. And many of the summits are high enough for it to be necessary to put on all the clothes you've got to come down.

But these lower passes don't seem to encourage this disregard and you have the warmth and leisure to appreciate the fall of the light through the trees - and above all the colour.

Quite the most colourful day I have ever spent on a bicycle. This is the Col de Rousset in France's Vercors Regional Park. On the map the road rises in a tantalisingly intricate series of close-packed hairpin bends from the little wine-producing town of Die. On the ground, the road winds up from the lower vineyards and pine forests through an incredible mass of laburnum flowers to the summit, close under spectacular and intimidating limestone crags. From the top the whole pattern of winding hairpins shows up as it sweeps away down to the valley, with a backdrop of range upon range of the hills of the Préalpes du Sud as far as the eye can see.

Our last journey of the book and a day I remember as probably the most enjoyable I have ever spent. We were on tour in early June in the Alps and had decided to spend two nights at Bourg d'Oisans so that we could strike up to the twin cols of Glandon and Croix de Fer. After a short stretch of almost flat road past the village of Oz, the climbing begins in earnest. With no more than

gentle bends and with no concessions to legs that have not yet warmed to their task the road rears up among spring birch trees past spectacular waterfalls, ice-cold as the streams are swollen with the season's melting snows. At the last hamlet, le Rivier, the gradient eases for a while and the character of the country changes. High to the left and right rocky snow-covered crags rear up while the trees abruptly cease. Ahead lies the Défilé de Maupas, a deep bare cleft with the road appearing to cling precariously to its left flank. For a while there is no shelter from the strengthening sun and then the road dives into a small birch copse and climbs sharply. When it emerges there are banks of snow in the deeper gullies by the side of the road. About a mile more of climbing and the road opens out into the Combe d'Olle. Once more the whole character has changed. This is a deep round-bottomed valley, grassy floored with the hitherto plunging torrent almost meandering along the centre. Here is an upland Alpine meadow, flower-strewn. We lunch by a clear stream and press on past the increasing snowdrifts and the mass of delicate mauve-lined crocus that seem to spring up from the very snow. There is a fork in the road: the left turn climbs a few yards to reach the 1924-metre summit of the Col du Glandon, the right leads between higher snow-banks to the 2068-metre Croix de Fer, with welcome hot chocolate at the summit refuge. Eastwards lies a tremendous spread of mountains across the valley of the Arc leading to the highest summits of the Alps.

A last, perhaps wistful, glance towards these summits and the descent begins, sweeping rapidly down past the landmarks we had so laboriously noted as we passed - the first and last crocus, the stream where we had lunched, the almost domestic pool with kingcups and then one of those tremendous surprises which is so much part of cycle-touring. The snow tunnel at one of the gullies, cold and forbiddingly in shadow as we came up, is ablaze in the afternoon sun, a golden gate leading back into the warmth of the valley below.

More about the photographs

Here is some more information about the photographs — principally where they were taken, as nearly as memory and the maps to hand will allow. For British pictures the Ordnance Survey 4-figure Grid Reference is given, specifying the spot to within a kilometre square. For French and Swiss locations, the Michelin map reference is given — to the nearest two kilometres — as follows: the first number is the Michelin 1:200 000 map sheet number, the second the fold number as marked on the map, the third the distance in centimetres from the left side of the map fold, and the fourth the distance in centimetres from the top of the fold or the top margin of the printed map if less. It sounds complex but it's the generally agreed system and it works. All the entries here are in page order: the bold numbers are the book page numbers.

1 Near Sallen, Calvados, Normandy, France, one Easter (Michelin 54-14-6-14).

2 Summer Heath near Turville, Buckinghamshire, in the southern Chilterns (GR SU 7490)

7 Villa-la-Sage, Val d'Herens, Valais, Switzerland, looking towards Arolla and Mt Blanc de Cheilon (3873 metres). (Michelin 26-3-6-2)

8/9 At Capelle-St-Josse, Somme, France (Michelin 51-11-6-13) — but it could be anywhere! A lith derivative from a black-and-white negative.

10 A contrast-enhanced Sabattier-effect multiple print from a lith derivative of a colour transparency! The original was taken on a cliff path near Sheringham, Norfolk, which seems scarcely relevant.

11 Cheating to some extent — but entirely photographically. The cyclists and road signs (now no longer there) were beside the Burway climb on the Long Mynd from Church Stretton in Shropshire; the mountains were near Achnasheen in the Scottish Highlands.

12/13 Near Vertuelle on the southern side of the Montagne de Reims, Marne, France (Michelin 56-17-1-8)

14 On the Quantock Hills ridge track in Somerset (GR ST 1635)

15 Near Great Hampden in the Buckinghamshire Chilterns in January (GR SP 8301)

16 A home-built chassis — rigid with the bicycle frame and riding like a lop-sided tricycle — supports a commercially-built Watsonian sidecar body, now no longer made.

17 In the Hafren Forest, Powys (GR SN 8686)

18 Near Brown Clee Hill, Shropshire (GR SO 6083)

19 West Harling Heath, near Thetford, Norfolk (GR TL 9583)

20 Easter at the Roche d'Oëtre in the Gorges de St Aubert of the River Orne, which is here the boundary between the départements of Orne and Calvados in Normandy, France (Michelin 55-11-8-22)

21 Looking westwards from the Roman Road over the Brecon Beacons, Powys (see also page **48**). (GR SO 0319)

22/23 Looking south over Llyn Brianne on the new Towy valley road, Powys. The river here forms the boundary between Powys and Dyfed. (GR SN 8054)

24/25 Near Erwood, Powys in February (GR SO 0844)

26 By the Strachur to Otter Ferry road beside Loch Fyne, Argyll (now part of the Strathclyde Region) (GR NR 9690)

27 Near Hawkshaw, off upper Tweeddale (now part of the Borders Region) (GR NT 0819)

28/29 Aldbury, Hertfordshire (GR SP 9612)

30 Upper photograph: near East Ruston, Norfolk (GR TG 3527) Lower photograph: boarding the ferry across the River Ouse at West Lynn, Norfolk (GR TF 6120)

31 Near Ryston, Downham Market, Norfolk (GR TF 6302)

32/33 Aldbury Common, Hertfordshire (GR SP 9711)

34 Three Shires Head — the meeting point of Cheshire, Staffordshire and Derbyshire in the Peak District National Park (GR SK 0068)

35 In the Brecon Forest on the Erwood-Brecon road, Powys (GR SO 0538)

36/37 Water Houses, near Kirkby Stephen, Cumbria (GR NY 7110)

38 Near Brockweir in the Wye Valley on the Gloucestershire/Gwent border (GR SO 5301)

39 Stainforth Bridge, North Yorkshire (GR SD 8167)

40/41 Chwar Blaen-Onneu on Mynydd Llangattock, Powys (GR SO 1516)

H.G. Wells's novel *The Wheels of Chance* is available in the Dent 'Everyman Library' series.